# The Other Side of Addiction

### Finding self-empowerment and trust in a world of challenges and heartbreak

*By*

*Anne McKenna*

# The Other Side of Addiction

There are at least two sides to a story. Anne shares her side of a remarkable story as a wife and mother dealing with her spouse's addiction.

This leads her on a tough and inspiring journey of discovering self-empowerment and trust in a world of challenges and heartbreak to find peace on the other side of addiction.

Written by Anne McKenna

Edited by Esther Robinson

# Table of Contents

# Dedication

I would like to dedicate this book to every person and family member who have suffered or are suffering at the hands of the disease of addiction. There is hope and help available.

# Acknowledgments

I would like to acknowledge the people who have encouraged me to believe in this project when I so many times was going to give up on it. You know who you are.

Thank you!

# About the Author

Anne is a simple unassuming woman who has an immense passion to help people who suffer from addictions and those who have been or are being affected by this disease. She is a spiritual person and attributes all she has achieved in life by the grace of her higher power the God of her understanding. She has no desire other than to make Al-Anon Family Groups better known to the wider community as so many people don't know of its existence including a lot of medical professionals. Her only aim is to create an awareness of the power of working the 12th Step programme (adapted from Alcoholic Anonymous) can have on a family members life whether their loved is in recovery or not. They say that if one person in a family unit gets help whether it be the person in addiction or a family member that this can stop addiction going on to the next generation. Anne feels that we owe it to our children the innocent victims of this disease to do all we can to recover from it's affects. This programme makes us better parents and grandparents by simply learning to mind our own business. As one AA member said one night if we mind our own business, we have a business to mind. Anne believes if someone like herself can change her life from where she came from anyone can do it with a bit of hard work, discipline and a simple desire to live a better more peaceful life.

# Introduction

I am a therapist and Al-Anon Family Groups member who has dealt with the effects of living with someone else's addiction successfully. As you have opened this book, so too have I opened my heart to share my story to give comfort, hope and inspiration to family members who are living with or have lived with someone struggling with overcoming addiction, as well as to assist the professionals who are working with them. I hope that my book will help many people, but even if this book helps only one person, it has served its purpose because a life transformed is a miracle.

Addiction is causing a great deal of damage in society. Addiction takes lives daily without any outcry from the public to do something about it. Years ago, I wrote an article for a local magazine in which I described addiction as a socially acceptable disease, and sadly, nothing has changed. I dream of the readers of this book gaining insights, understanding and toolkit for healing that I share by weaving them throughout my story.

I am grateful to have met the man who became my husband since it was because of him that I availed of the life-changing 'Al-Anon Family Group's Twelve Steps'[1] programme.

There was no pattern of addiction in my family while I was growing up that I may have taken on as a learned behaviour, yet I was told by my doctor six-and-a-half years into my marriage that I was living with a person who had a drinking problem without having recognised it.

I dive into my vulnerability to explore emotions such as denial, shame, guilt, anger, resentment, grief and loss, which are symptoms of the disease of addiction. I look at the different roles that are common in dysfunctional families. I describe what sponsorship is. I discuss the importance of self-care and include some phrases and prayers to help people change their mindset from one of negativity to positivity, encouraging them to take pauses and time for daily reflection, live at a slower and more self-aware pace, and learn to live one day at a time with gratitude.

I am not a spokesperson for Al-Anon Family Groups or 'Twelve Steps of Alcoholics Anonymous' recovery programmes, but I describe how I incorporated this recovery programme into my life because it not only saved my life but helped me create a new one that is far more fulfilling than I could have ever imagined it would be. You can make that happen, too.

The opinions expressed in this book are my own and are drawn from my experience in my personal and professional life. I have changed the names of the people in my book to protect their privacy.

# CHAPTER ONE
# Monaghan Roots

My name is Anne. I was born in County Monaghan in the Republic of Ireland in 1960.

I was reared on a farm outside the village of Emyvale with my six siblings and my parents.

Our familial relationships and circumstances shape our lives much the same way as the elements forge the landscape around us. We were all so connected with the land and nature, for which I still have a great appreciation, as it's where peace can be found.

Everything changed when I was 10, when my father, John, died from lung cancer.

# CHAPTER TWO
# My Father

My father, John, was a tall, strong and handsome man. He passed away at the age of 55 after battling lung cancer for over a year. He was a lot older than my mother, Agnes. He was very proud of her and their children. He was a hard-working man and what they would have called in those days a 'progressive farmer'.

John loved music and dancing. My mother would say that when they went to the local dances, he would 'dance her all night'. He brought my two sisters and I to Irish dancing classes every Sunday at 3 pm in Aughnacloy, Co. Tyrone. While we danced, he visited our family's good friends, Laura and Monica Brady or the Haddens. He took one of my brothers to accordion classes every Friday night. We really did not appreciate the opportunities we were given then or the effort our dad made to create them for us while immersing us into our Irish culture. None of us were 'River Dance' material, but if we had visitors, we would have to step it out on the kitchen floor for them as our parents looked on proudly.

My father was a staunch member of the National Farmers' Association (NFA) and stood up for farmers' rights. He was a man who said what he thought. He would turn in his grave, watching what had happened to our local Town of Monaghan Co-op. Established in 1901 and renowned for stocking top-quality dairy products from 300 farmers – including my father – and supporting community events, it became unrecognisable through a merger in 2015. Sometimes, when things become focused too much on commercialism, they lose their heart and some of their soul. I prefer community to be at the heart of things rather than commercialism. But part of life is accepting that things can change whether we want them to or not, for worse or better. It is how we react and adapt to change that is important.

I have many happy memories of my father. He'd often play with us. He put up a swing for us and made a seesaw out of a barrel and a plank of wood. He stood up for us if the teacher did not treat us right. He brought us all to the seaside at Blackrock in the summertime in his VW Beetle. On the way, we ate a picnic that our mother had made, and it tasted so delicious.

On 8$^{th}$ December, we all headed to town after Mass to do the Christmas shopping. We all got a new toy from the toy shop that day and Mum did the Santa shopping. Dad had a bottle of Guinness in Bobby Loan's where he would get tickets for us to go to see Santa at Monaghan Courthouse when Santa came for his annual visit.

No one told us that our father had a terminal illness. I guess it was out of some sense of protecting us from worry and grief. When we did realise he was unwell, we still had no idea how seriously ill he was. I remember the first time the ambulance came to take him to the hospital in Dublin. John came home a few times after that, with a little less of him each time as he was losing weight and his hair from the chemotherapy.

I remember the day my father died. It was a lovely summer day on 23$^{rd}$ June 1971. I went home from school and walked straight upstairs to the wee room that was off the landing where we played, but it was full of objects that usually resided in other rooms in the house. It was as if these items had rudely decided to take up squatters' rights in my special place while I was out for the day. Affronted and puzzled, I went downstairs to ask my mother what all the stuff was doing in the playroom when she told me that she had moved items because my father had died. At that age, I did not understand the finality of my father's absence as I had gotten used to him not being around for some time due to his hospital stays. I did not display any grief because it didn't dawn on me at that time that my expectation of seeing him again soon would never be met. I went out through what we called the back house and met a neighbour coming into my house. I found it odd that instead of simply saying hello to me and passing by like he normally would have done, he shook my hand formally.

My mother then told me to go with my two younger brothers to my uncle's house and mind them there, so I gathered their things together, and we headed off. I remember watching the sunlight dance on the river as we gleefully caught little fish with jam jars by his house as if nothing out of the ordinary was happening at home.

My father was well respected in the local area, and his funeral was one of the most well-attended at that time.

# CHAPTER THREE
# My Mother

My mother, Agnes, was born in Co. Cavan. She was employed as a legal secretary in Aughnacloy when she met my father. They met at the Glaslough Fete in Co. Monaghan when he offered to ride his bicycle gallantly in front of my mother and her friend through Emyvale, which was a good bit out of his way, as neither my mother nor her friend had a light on their bicycles, which I think was an offence in those days. When they were parting company after the fete, John asked Agnes if there were any dances in Aughnacloy, and she replied that there was one in a week or so but not to blame her if it was no good. My father turned up at the dance and they were together up until my father's death. It must have been a good dance.

My mother was brought up on a farm but had little interest in it, but somehow, she coped with being a farmer's wife with the help of good neighbours. Agnes worked extremely hard and was a gifted dressmaker who made most of our clothes and knit a lot of our jumpers and cardigans. She also made our dancing costumes and embroidered them by hand, straining her eyes and fighting off any cramp that threatened to thwart her creativity into the small hours of the night to have them ready for the Fèish in Dungannon, Co. Tyrone. I used to hate to see the sewing machine come out as it became my mother's sole companion while everyone and everything else was put to one side until her masterpiece was completed.

She is to this day a great sewer and baker with visitors delighting in her soda and currant bread, all made with her instinctively accurate sense of quantities and no weighing or measuring utensils employed.

Nothing pleased my mother more than getting away for the day to her native Cavan, where her two brothers and her sisters-in-law still live. Essential activities on these visits include popping into the bakery for her favourite apple tarts, some shopping and enjoying lunch in the Farnham Arms Hotel.

My mother was just learning to drive when my father became ill because circumstances forced her to become more independent, and this was a big step for her.

My mother is a strong, determined woman who has had to cope with two major losses in her life: my father's death when she was about 40 and the loss of her daughter, my sister, 20 years ago.

# CHAPTER FOUR
# School Days

I never really liked school, so I volunteered to be the 'little caretaker' at home for any reason I could find, especially to look after my younger brothers with my eldest brother when my mother and father had to go somewhere.

I always struggled with reading, writing and spelling. I had dyslexia, which was not a well-known or widely recognised learning disability in those days. You were either classed as smart or stupid, and I often felt I was the latter.

Edenmore was a country school with four teachers. Sadly, there are few happy memories from my time at this school. Some of our teachers may have been more suited to another career. In the schoolyard, I must admit with shame and regret that I did some bullying myself when disputes arose between pupils from the two parishes that attended our school. But we all learn right from wrong through experience.

After finishing national school, I attended the tech – now Beech Hill College – in Monaghan town as there were better opportunities there to get a trade involving more hands-on learning, which I found easier than academic learning. I loved home economics and was particularly good at it and I was also good at art. If I did an oral exam, I was not too bad at it, but if I had to do a written exam, that was another story.

I enjoyed secondary school, but with the Group and Inter Cert looming, I was getting itchy feet. I had been shamed by my English teacher in front of the whole class when she accused me of not learning an English poem. I had learned it and knew that poem by heart at home the evening before, but I couldn't remember it in class. I was so hurt by the teacher's remarks that I cried in front of the class as she had no idea about the effort I had put into learning it, my frustration at not being able to remember it the next day and that I had been so happy with my achievement only a few hours before. Poor retention is now recognised as another indication of dyslexia. The change in the approach of educators towards children with dyslexia today is one change that is most welcome, and a pity it did not come sooner.

I had spent two weeks working in our friends Laura and Monica Brady's draper shop in Aughnacloy the summer before I was due to turn 15, and this planted the seed about finding a job in a shop as my career because I enjoyed it and could do it efficiently. In those days, believe it or not, you had to complete a three-year apprenticeship to qualify as a shop assistant. My mother was not happy about my decision because she wanted us all to have an education like herself. She went into the tech to speak to my year teacher. They both wanted me to stay at school, but I was afraid of failing my exams. So, I was told I had to find a job before I could leave school, so I eagerly set about looking for a post. I couldn't believe my luck when a job opportunity arose for a trainee shop assistant in Monaghan town. I applied for it and I was delighted and relieved when I was given the job shortly after my fifteenth birthday, like a belated birthday gift. It felt like I was finally getting somewhere in my life.

# CHAPTER FIVE
# Career Steps

My first job was in the draper shop in Monaghan town when I was 15. I enjoyed the work and felt settled there. I am still good friends with one of the owners and their family to this day. Unfortunately, the shop closed down about 18 months later, so I had to find another job. The universe was still calling me to deal with change.

I set out from home and walked a couple of miles to the main road from where I thumbed a lift into Monaghan town. Thumbing lifts were safe and commonplace then, but not like today. I felt a heady mix of apprehension and hope rising in my gut as I walked from one end of the town to the other, stopping at every shop along the way to ask if they needed any staff. I felt dejected when I was told that I had just missed a few job opportunities and was kicking myself that I hadn't gone into town before today.

A feeling of hopelessness began to weave its way around my heart as I sloped back out of the town to thumb a lift home. As I was waiting, a passing car pulled up alongside me. It was driven by the owner of a supermarket, which was the first shop I had walked into that morning. She asked me if I'd had any luck finding work. I couldn't hide my disappointment. Perhaps she felt sorry for me knowing how long I had spent in town job hunting, or she knew I'd lost my job at the draper shop through no fault of my own, or she had a change of heart, or an opportunity had suddenly arisen because she offered me a job and I accepted gratefully. The huge smile that spread across my face seemed to make her face light up. I couldn't wait to go home and tell my mother I had found a new job. Perhaps divine timing was at play after all. I got along well with the other staff at the supermarket and enjoyed working there, but the lure of better pay elsewhere meant I only stayed in that role for six months.

My next post was in a shoe factory not far from my home. After completing the six weeks of training, my first task was making boxes or packing shoes. But I soon grew weary of the regimental way of working by the clock. If you completed the task in a shorter time, you earned a bonus. But it felt as if I was working like a robot, not a human being. Always doing rather than being is not good for the soul. Many of the shoe factory floor workers, including me, were collected from their homes around the countryside in a black minibus, which felt to me like being rounded up to be brought to prison in a 'Black Maria' for the day. My spirit died a little each day I was there.

Of all the jobs that I have ever done, I disliked this one the most. Towards the end of the six weeks' training, I saw an advertisement in the local newspaper for a shop assistant in one of the best draper shops in Monaghan town. After a successful informal interview with the owner the following Saturday, I accepted the job. I had been earning £30 per week in the shoe factory, so I had to make some adjustments in my budget to go back to living on £15 per week at the draper shop. But I was much happier there, and this was my first lesson in understanding that money couldn't buy you happiness or fulfilment.

A decade later, I was still content in this role, but I had to hand in my notice because I was going to become a stay-at-home mum. This new role would be non-stop with no pay and would initiate some of the biggest transitions in my life.

# CHAPTER SIX
# At the Threshold of Roses and Thorns

In 1978, I met Robert, the man I was going to marry. I wished my father could have met my husband. I often wondered what they would think of each other. My husband was and still is a hard worker and always worked long hours. My father would definitely have approved of Robert's work ethic as he had been a hard worker, too. My fiancé was kind and generous, and there was an element of excitement and fun about him making up for my dull lifestyle. We got married in 1982 when we were both young and thought we knew it all.

I wanted us to own our own house, so I was happy to deal with everything at home to allow Robert to work long hours to save up a deposit. We felt so excited and proud of ourselves when we achieved this, but on my first shopping trip to Belfast, our car got stolen, and because of a mix-up with the insurance, we didn't get compensation, so our deposit had to go towards another car.

When Robert's parents decided to move out of their cottage in the country to move into the local village for convenience, we moved into the cottage. This is where my husband had been reared. I loved that cottage and its pretty setting, with an abundance of beautiful red roses growing up the front of the house, greeting us with their intoxicating fragrance as we went in and out of our home. I'd breathe in that sweet scent, and it would infuse my heart with love and the glow of optimism that only a summer's day can bring.

We had been married for over three years and had been living in the cottage for about one month when our first child, Joe, was born. This was a very happy time in our lives. I loved being a stay-at-home mum and having the time and freedom to go for long walks with our baby, who I proudly transported about in a new bright red buggy.

I was back at work full-time by the time Joe was three months old because you didn't get long on maternity leave in those days. When we both worked full-time, we only had a short time to spend with Joe in the evenings before his early bedtime, and none of us were happy about that. I went part-time when he was one year old and then gave up work completely when he was about 18 months old, as Robert was still working long hours.

We decided that we would like another child. My second pregnancy was completely different from the first as I experienced more morning sickness. Robert got a different job, and he was now working longer hours, which meant I was on my own with Joe much more, and it wasn't easy tending to him while I felt unwell.

The local hospital had two days assigned per week for delivering babies, so if a baby happened to be born naturally before those days, the mother was lucky. Otherwise, all expectant mothers had their labour induced on or around either of those designated days, which resulted in a great deal of unnecessary pain in childbirth as well as suffering and trauma after the birth.

Our second child's due date coincided with one of the designated delivery days, so he was induced that day, and we named him Fabian. Our first child had been induced, too. It was Shrove Tuesday, a day I would normally be at home making pancakes. After Fabian's delivery, every time a doctor or nurse checked up on me, they would comment, 'You are very bruised'. I didn't know what they were talking about until around three weeks after the birth when I caught a glimpse of my back in the mirror and saw that it was black and blue with extensive bruises. The physical trauma was evident, but the hospital staff didn't perceive the psychological damage I was experiencing from my childbirth experience.

I remember the day I got out of the hospital when my husband, with our first child, came to collect me. I felt happy to be getting home, but a strange feeling of apprehension had descended upon me. The next day, I remember my good friend and neighbour calling to see me and taking Joe over to her house, so I could have time to myself with my newborn. I was so grateful to her as I knew I was struggling to cope with daily activities, which was not like me as I had always been so independent, never needing any help from other people. This new territory of feeling helpless and codependent was not one I wanted to explore, but I felt like I was being forced on a journey that I was powerless to halt. I had been married for six-and-a-half years by this time and had never needed my husband's support before. But I felt that I needed his help now as I was finding it a challenge to meet Joe's needs, while Fabian needed so much of my time and energy, too. I seemed to be in a constant cycle of flitting from feeding both of them and changing nappies.

Getting less sleep made everything feel like more of a struggle. I felt more emotional and less resilient. Robert and I began to have rows about the amount of time he was away from home. This continued for about the next eight months until I went to see a doctor in the south of Ireland. I didn't visit my own GP as I had a fear that her assessing my state of mind might result in her sending Social Services to investigate me if they thought I could not cope. It was getting more difficult to keep my frustration in check, which resulted in outbursts of anger, which I then felt guilty about and I got angry with myself, sending me into an ever-deepening spiral of negativity.

This doctor's sympathy and understanding extended to him, telling me that his wife would like to have him at home more, too, and he prescribed me some medication. But I decided not to take it and made up my mind that next year would be different. I made a New Year resolution that this year we would spend more quality time together as a family, but – like so many resolutions with the best of intentions – this didn't come to fruition.

After a disastrous Easter break in Dublin spent visiting my sister, I decided that I would seek out a counsellor to talk to. I remember going into town, dropping our children off with my sister and crying all the way to the counsellor's office and throughout the appointment. The counsellor was a nice lady, but when I talked about my home life, she did not recognise the signs of addiction there. She advised me to go to my own GP about my inability to sleep.

I found courage one Tuesday morning and went to see my own GP and told her that when my husband left the house in the morning the frustration in me was so high that I felt like breaking every window in the house with a stone. The way I saw it at that time was that Robert had the freedom to come and go as he liked, whereas I felt I was left at home with our children without my freedom. She turned around to me and asked, 'You do realise that you are living with a person with a drinking problem?' and I nearly fell off the chair.

I had always thought that living with a drinking problem was something I would not put up with, and here I was, living with it. I never saw the drinking, and, to this day, I do not know how much or how often Robert was drinking. But it was the frequent absence of

Robert that left me feeling isolated and with too much to cope with on my own that had far-reaching consequences.

I went home and told Robert what the GP had said, and I suppose neither of us really believed it. I had known married couples dealing with a drinking problem that was very evident, but that was not the case in our home. Perhaps I had become so consumed with my own pain that I had become blind to the pain of others and what was going on around me.

I now know that I was suffering from post-traumatic stress disorder from the birth of our second child, which was never diagnosed, which would account for the change in my personality and the anger I felt and projected onto those around me. I am sure that I was not the only mother in the county that suffered in the same way with no help or understanding of the effect of trauma on the mind and body. Today, in my role as a counsellor, in every assessment I complete with a mother, I ask about her experience of childbirth, and most of them have a story to tell involving some form of trauma.

By the end of the week, things had got worse. I cannot remember what had happened, but I phoned the doctor and asked her where I could go to get help. She said that she would put me in touch with an Al-Anon Family Groups member who lived locally and suggested that I go to a meeting with this woman. I did not know what Al-Anon Family Groups were. Alcoholics Anonymous was co-founded by Bill Wilson. His wife Lois and some other women co-founded the Al-Anon Family Groups as a type of sister fellowship of Alcoholics Anonymous when these wives of alcoholics realised that they also needed support. The story is portrayed in the 2010 film, *'When Love Is Not Enough: The Lois Wilson Story'*. The Al-Anon Family Groups adopted the *'Twelve Steps of Alcoholics Anonymous'*.[1]

I felt desperate and plucked up the courage to contact the local woman from the Al-Anon Family Groups, who kindly offered to accompany me to a meeting on Sunday evening. I had to organise a babysitter, and I remember the children crying when I was leaving the house as I never went anywhere without them. I felt guilty but knew I had to walk out that door to try to improve our home life, although I was also curious to find out if my GP was right about my husband having a drinking problem because I still could hardly believe it. Before I went to Al-Anon Family Groups I felt like I was losing my mind. I had no gratitude in my life. I felt like I was living in a black hole. When I lost my temper with our two young children, I would feel so guilty. It was this anger and guilt that prompted me to seek help. I told my children that mammy was going to a meeting to stop being cross with them as they were my victims. As I stepped out of the front door, I glanced back and realised I was taking my first step towards a new life. A new life that would materialise when I took a further 'Twelve Steps'.

# CHAPTER SEVEN
# Support from a Sponsor

Sponsorship is often mentioned throughout the books on addiction recovery and in the recovery meetings. It is an especially important part of the recovery journey. A sponsor is a person who has been in recovery longer than the person they are helping, and they have proved they are implementing a good recovery programme in their own lives, particularly within their own family.

It is someone that can give a consistent ear to a newcomer in the programme. I suggest to new members to obtain phone numbers of willing members that they feel could help them. Personal life experiences are best shared with a sponsor who can keep matters confidential, and this is often the beginning of a meaningful friendship. They will also expect those they sponsor to respect their confidences. It is suggested that you have a sponsor of the same sex as yourself, unless you are gay, to help prevent any emotional attachment.

Sponsors need to be attending their own recovery meetings and have regular interaction with their own sponsors. A sponsor will expect those they sponsor to attend their recovery meetings and keep in regular contact with them. This is where we learn to ask for help, something I had not been good at. Sponsors will give tough love at times and suggestions, but they will not give direct advice. This is an opportunity to feel what feels right for you and to learn to trust your own judgement.

It is a privilege to be able to progress to become a sponsor for someone else once a good grasp of the recovery programme has been obtained. Through seeking help, we are then able to offer assistance.

# CHAPTER EIGHT
# Walking in My Shoes

These are the steps I had to take to walk away from an old life and walk my way into a new one. The Twelve Steps[1] programme is a spiritual programme that works for all faiths or none. It is a belief in a higher power of your own understanding. My Al-Anon sponsor walked these steps with me as much as she could, and now I walk you through how I applied them in my life and how they can help transform your life for the better.

**Step 1**: 'We admitted we were powerless over alcohol – that our lives had become unmanageable.'

This can apply to drugs, gambling or whatever the addiction may be. People, places and situations should also be included in this. All of which we have no power over. Step one is the most important of all the 12 Steps, as without accepting this step, all the rest of them will have no meaning. It would be like trying to climb up stairs that crumble under your feet because there is no solid foundation on which to build. If a person has any notion that someday in the future, they will be able to control a substance or gambling or behaviour, they have not accepted the powerlessness of step one. If a family member believes they have the power to change another person, they, too, have not accepted step one.

The most important word in this initial step is the first one, 'We', which tells us that a person cannot recover from this disease on their own regardless of whether they are the addict or the family member. While family members of a person dealing with addiction can offer a great deal of support and advice to help the addict deal with their disease, that person has to want to change. Family members affected by the addiction can only change when they understand what addiction is and how it has affected them. At that time, it was a relief for me to finally get to the root of the problem and to understand that I was powerless to fix it. I had learned that the only person I could change was myself. As you transform yourself, you will see those changes reflected in the people around you. According to Rehab UK[2] approximately another five people will be affected by one addict, and often, it also has a ripple effect in the community. I personally feel that one person in active addiction can affect up to at least 20 people directly.

One of the hardest parts of this step as a parent is to accept that your children will always have some struggles in life and that you can't change your children as much as you love them and want to save them from the hurts of this world. It is a lot harder to detach from them. The award-winning journalist and essayist Elizabeth Stone said: 'Making the decision to have a child – it is momentous. It is to decide forever to have your heart go walking around outside your body'. This will especially ring true for the parents of a child or children experiencing addiction. Most people will accept that in trying to change other people their own life becomes unmanageable.

**Step 2**: 'Came to believe that a Power greater than ourselves could restore us to sanity.'

This step is often called the step of hope. Insanity is described in 'The Big Book' of AA as doing the same thing over and over, expecting different results. Show me a person in addiction who cannot relate to this or a family member who is desperate to get their family member into recovery. When we hear about all the unmanageable and dangerous situations that people get themselves into, and they are still here to tell the tale, I believe some power greater than themselves was looking after them.

I always explain the second step backwards and ask people if they believe that they have done some insane things through their addiction or while living with it. I did some insane things like driving my car erratically with my two children in the back seat when I was so angry I was no saner or safer than a drunk driver. Addicts are stereotyped as getting drunk or high on a substance or behavioural pattern, but family members of addicts can get drunk or high on emotions. I believe some higher power looked after me on those dark days, enabling me to somehow function and look after our children. I believe that this higher power brought me to Al-Anon. Without the 'Twelve Steps'[1] programme and the people I met through it, I might not be here today.

**Step 3:** 'Made a decision to turn our will and our lives over to the care of God *as we understood Him.*'

The most important words in this step are 'made a decision' because if you do not make the decision to turn your will and your life over, you are still acting in self-will, which hasn't worked in the past. People in addiction ask for help to keep clean, sober and free from gambling. The part about God *as we understood Him* is important as everybody has the freedom to choose their interpretation of what God is to them or what their higher power is. Some people think of the God they were brought up with if they were a loving God, or they might see it as a force of 'Good Orderly Direction (G.O.D.)' or it may be their recovery group, nature, the universe, their guardian angel or a close relative that has passed away. The most important thing is to use your higher power. It takes practice until it becomes part of your daily routine to help you have a good day and to be open to the journey that your higher power has in store for you.

The third step means that when you take the time to surrender your will and life over to your higher power in the morning, it creates a peaceful acceptance within you that whatever happens that day is meant to happen in the way it happens. Before Al-Anon, I operated on thick wit and ignorance. If I had a plan for the day, by hook or by crook, I would try to achieve whatever it was and whatever it took, and our poor children suffered in the middle of it. This step is often described as the difference between flowing down the stream of life or facing the current. The first three steps are about giving up our illusion of control. Most people in recovery find this to be a relief.

In the past, AA members were told to put their shoes under the bed at night and in the morning, when they got down on their knees to reach their shoes, that is when they handed their day over. But it is not about humiliation. It's about humility and having a true desire to receive help throughout your day and to be open to receiving it.

A lot of people struggle with the concept of a higher power. It can be anything you choose it to be if you believe that it is there to love you unconditionally, guide you to do the right thing, be willing to ask for its will to be done in your life daily and be willing to accept whatever is to come. A higher power has often been referred to as being like electricity. You don't need to know where electricity comes from to enjoy the benefits of it. You just need to turn on the switch and welcome the light to diminish the darkness. A higher power will only work to the level at which you connect with it.

I asked for help, and after a few months in Al-Anon, my prayers were answered, which gave me the confidence to hand my will and my life over to the care of my higher power, who is the God of my understanding. My own will had made a mess of my life, so I trusted that my higher power would make things better.

**Step 4**: 'Made a searching and fearless moral inventory of ourselves.'

In this step, you are asked to spend time looking into your own life, reflecting on it and journalling about it. Al-Anon Family Groups published a book called the 'Blueprint for Progress'[3] to use. The name itself says a lot. Your blueprint is what you were before all your life experiences changed you. To me, this is about reclaiming who you would like to be by letting go of the past. You are ready to do this step when you are working the first three steps automatically and when the fourth step starts to bother you. It is also good to ask your higher power to help you remember all parts of your life to be sure not to leave anything out. Other recovery groups have their own way of completing step four.

Few people ever take the time to stop and examine their lives or to get to know who they really are in terms of their defects, gifts and talents. They live on autopilot. For me, this step was one of self-discovery and honesty. I used to think of myself as a victim, and I had to change this attitude. Many people do not do this step out of fear of what they may discover about themselves, but, as the saying goes, you may discover that you are not half as bad as you thought you were. When I completed this step, I had already begun to change into a person that I was beginning to like. I was also sharing what was coming up for me with my sponsor as I went along. This is the step you do for yourself, so it should not be rushed, as it is the most worthwhile time you will ever spend.

**Step 5**: 'Admitted to God, to ourselves, and to another human being the exact nature of our wrongs.'

With step five looming, you can see why step four often never gets started. Professor and author Brené Brown said: 'Our stories are

25

not meant for everyone. Hearing them is a privilege, and we should always ask ourselves this before we share: "Who has earned the right to hear my story?"[4]

That eliminates a lot of people. It takes courage to share your life story with someone. God or our higher power already knows our story, but I believe the essence of this step is getting rid of your shame and getting acceptance, maybe for the first time in your life. Brené Brown says that shame is enabled to grow in an environment of 'secrecy, silence and judgement' and the biggest judge you will meet in life is yourself. She also said: "'When we tell our stories or share an experience with someone, and they respond with empathy, most of our shame loses its power.'"[5]

The person that you choose to listen to your step five should be somebody who you trust completely and has earned the right to hear your story. They are often a person's sponsor. Many people have said that this was the first relationship in their life in which they experienced intimacy. Intimacy = 'into me you see'. This means being able to open up to another person. This is allowing someone to really see you, being vulnerable, with all your flaws. Some choose a clergyman or woman or their therapist. I have had the privilege to hear people's step fives. It is then that you hear the pain and shame that people carry all their lives up to this moment.

Pastor Rick Warren said: 'You're only as sick as your secrets.' So, step five is your chance to get rid of them and leave them behind you. Keeping secrets is the cause of many people's relapse. I always encouraged my clients to leave their secrets in the treatment centre or therapy session because keeping them poses a danger to their recovery.

Shame disconnects people. People wear masks because they worry that others will not like the real person behind the mask. In my lectures, I often ask how many people isolate themselves during their addiction, and 20 hands would go up in the room. People in active addiction isolate in their shame, and so do family members. Step five gives us an invitation to let this shame go and discover all the assets that lie underneath our defects.

**Step 6**: 'Were entirely ready to have God remove all these defects of character.'

After completing step five, we start to become aware of some of our not-so-nice traits, and now we are getting ready to have God or a higher power remove them. Mine included blaming everybody else, especially my poor husband, for everything that went wrong. It was always someone else's fault. While I had one finger pointing out, there were three fingers pointing back at me. Blame is the stick we use to beat up others. In recovery, I learned to take responsibility for my part in any situation and own my own mistakes.

The other big defect I discovered I had was being sarcastic. I thought this was a funny trait to have until I learned the meaning of the word sarcasm in Al-Anon Family Groups. It comes from the Greek verb 'sarkazein', which means 'to tear flesh'. Not such a nice trait now! Being sarcastic is a bit like throwing out a boomerang, and then it comes back and takes the head off you, as you must live with the consequences of whatever ugly words you send out. This trait is related to our own shame and anger. Other defects I had included holding on to resentment, being a people pleaser at the expense of myself and not being able to mind my own business. I had an opinion on everything and everybody. All my defects were causing me a lot of damage.

**Step 7**: 'Humbly asked Him to remove our shortcomings.'

Humility is something that is necessary for recovery. The ability to be able to ask for help is essential. It is often not something people like doing. I always ask people how they feel when someone asks them for help, and they mostly reply that it gives them a good feeling. So, I say that by not asking for help, you are depriving someone of feeling good. Step seven is the first step where we ask our higher power directly for something. To have our shortcomings removed, we must recognise them and then be willing to let them go by working on them one at a time. It is a bit like pulling weeds in the garden; the more you pull them, the less there are. It is hard to let go of shortcomings that have served you in the past. We wonder who we will be without them. I turned into a much better person without mine. I can look in the mirror and like and love the person who is looking back at me. This step is a work in progress.

**Step 8**: 'Made a list of all persons that we had harmed and became willing to make amends to them all.'

For this step, you must write a list of all the people you have harmed. It is not that easy to put the names of people down on paper that you know you have harmed, but the second part of this step about making amends means that by working the previous seven steps, you have already started the process of making amends. The word 'amend' comes from the Latin word 'emendare', which means 'to correct or free from fault', so change has already begun. I was no longer the angry mother who had no patience or put cleaning the house before spending quality time with our children, which made me more pleasant to be around. I treated myself and others with respect. Instead of saying 'no' all the time, I said 'maybe' or 'yes'.

Having already done a lot of work to let go of my resentments meant I had fewer people to add to the list at this stage. I was told in Al-Anon that in order to let go of the resentments I was carrying, I needed to pray for those people I felt resentment towards and ask my higher power to remove my bitter feelings. The first thing I had to do was to be willing to let them go and loosen my grip. During my lectures on resentments, I often told the residents that in the past, I had prayed for 17 people a night until all the resentments were gone and were replaced by compassion, understanding and gratitude. At that time, I missed out on one person who should have been first on that list, which was myself. It was a few years later that I prayed to have the resentments that I felt towards myself to be removed.

**Step 9**: 'Made direct amends to such people wherever possible, except when to do so would injure them or others.'

This step requires us to act, but not at the expense of others. When I made amends to our children, they did not remember their crazy mother, but I did. That is what keeps me in the recovery groups, as I have no desire to go back there. I started making amends to my husband after the first Al-Anon meeting when I discovered that he was suffering from a disease, not badness, and I continue to treat him with respect and compassion as the father of our children and as a person who has also suffered from his own life journey.

Years ago, when I was on my knees washing the carpet tiles in our cottage, I remember congratulating myself that I was at peace with the world when a thought came into my head. It was not a comfortable thought as it brought up guilt and shame in me for the way I behaved towards relatives on my father's side. Many families have an ongoing dispute that can last from one generation to the next, and ours was no different. With the new understanding and life experience that Al-Anon gave me, I could now look at this situation differently. There were wrongs on both sides of the family I am sure, but it was the way I behaved that brought a big chunk of guilt and shame that I knew I needed to make amends for and let the past go. I made up my mind there and then that the next time I saw them I was going to speak to them.

My higher power seems to have a sense of humour because, within two weeks, I received an invitation to a relative's 50th wedding anniversary party. That night, I decided if there was a chance to make amends, I would. The opportunity presented itself, and the family were receptive towards me. I do not know what they thought of me then or what they think of me now, but that is not important. What I had thought of them was damaging my peace of mind and serenity, which is why I had to change my thoughts towards them to more positive ones.

**Step 10:** 'Continued to take personal inventory and when we were wrong promptly admitted it.'

In step 10, we try to keep our slate clean after or even before we complete the previous nine steps. It is the step I practise nightly, in my prayer at the end of the day, in the same way, that I practise step three of surrendering my life and concerns to God each morning.

In step 10, I ask myself, did I see my higher power working through my day and did I listen to the prompting and inspirations that my higher power gave me? That could be to make a telephone call, bring in the washing, send that email or connect with someone who may need my support, etc. Then, I check if I need to make any amends for something I did or said that day that hurt someone when I was not my best self. I remember the first amends I made was to my dear mother-in-law for snapping at her for saying the wrong thing when I was in a foul mood. I phoned her and apologised for the way I had spoken to her because I knew she had meant well. It was a good habit that started that day. When you adopt this daily habit of making amends, you reap the benefits of serenity.

The last part of step 10 is to reflect on my day and see what I can be grateful for. I was inspired by talk show host Oprah Winfrey keeping a daily gratitude journal, which she said changed her life for the better. 'Gratitude changes your attitude' is my daily motto, and everyone that was in the treatment centre when I was there will testify to this. In the past, on a bad day, I knew I had so much to be grateful for, but I just could not feel it that day, and that's okay, too. At least I was acknowledging that I knew I still had things to be grateful for. I also hand any concerns I have over to my higher power and go to sleep, as I know my higher power is watching over me and helping to work things out on my behalf.

**Step 11:** 'Sought through prayer and meditation to improve our conscious contact with God *as we understood Him*, praying only for knowledge of His will for us and the power to carry that out.'

By the time I reached step 11, I had become more spiritually aware, noticing my higher power moments, listening to my gut feelings and practising mindfulness meditation while being more mindful in my day-to-day living. Prayer is an important part of my daily practice. Most of my prayers are for other people who are struggling with illnesses, etc. I pray with the kind of trust you have if you ask your best friend to do something for you. You would have faith that they would do their best for you, and so it is with my higher power. I learned to pray for guidance and acceptance. Sometimes I think I have fully surrendered and then He asks me to give up something I don't want to give up" How true this quote is to life, with all the losses people have to endure throughout their lives in this world. In step three, I ask daily to do my higher power's will to the best of my ability and I have been taken on a journey beyond my wildest dreams.

**Step 12**: 'Having had a spiritual awakening as the result of these steps, we tried to carry this message to others and practice these principles in all our affairs.'

I believe that step 12 is one of the promises of the 12 Step Recovery program.[1] It doesn't say that you 'might have had' a spiritual awakening. It states, 'having had a spiritual awakening', which I believe is where you find yourself as a result of the work you have completed. At this stage, you are free to be your authentic self and own your gifts and talents with the awareness that you are no better than or worse than any other person in the universe.

'We tried to carry the message to others' tells me that there are no mistakes in the way these steps are written. This part of the twelfth step assures us that there will always be someone with the door open at our recovery meetings for the newcomer (there was no plan when the coronavirus created a pandemic, but thankfully, we can use online meeting rooms to keep connecting with and motivating people). One of the principles of recovery is to maintain our state of recovery. We help others maintain their state of recovery in gratitude for those who helped us overcome our addiction or codependency.

'Practice these principles in all our affairs' is a tall order for us all to live by. Alcoholics Anonymous states that you keep your sobriety through 'rigorous honesty', which means being honest in all your affairs.

I would ask anyone living with addiction, whether active or not, to consider going to recovery meetings for the suggested six weeks to find out how they may be beneficial. When I went into Al-Anon over 30 years ago, I had no dreams, ambitions or goals. I was a wife and a mother of two young children, which I was content to be. But I gained a life beyond my wildest dreams – as promised in the recovery rooms – through hard work, discipline and a willingness to change by working 'Al-Anon's Twelve Steps'[1] of recovery in my life.

# CHAPTER NINE
# Al-Anon Family Groups

At my first Al-Anon Family groups meeting I was told that they used first names only to protect people's privacy and that everything discussed within the meeting was to be kept confidential. There was no hierarchy, and everyone took their turn to chair the meeting. I was told that alcoholism is a disease and that nobody would choose this disease if they had a choice. It could never be cured, but could be arrested one day at a time. It is a family disease because it doesn't just affect the individual who is drinking excessively but also the family. I listened to the women speaking and I could identify so much with what they were saying. Until that evening, I had thought I was the only person in the country who felt the way I did, but I was amazed to find so many other women in a similar situation to me. They were dealing with the same range of emotions, and it was a comfort to know I was not alone and that I would be able to talk to people who understood what I was going through.

I was also told about Al-Anon's 'Three Cs', which are: 'I didn't cause it, I can't control it, and I can't cure it'. I was also told that the only person I could change was myself. There was a leaflet entitled 'Is Al-Anon for you?' with 20 questions on it, and I could have answered 'yes' to a lot of them without being aware of the drinking. Today, I understand that even though Robert and I were not aware of the addiction, we both suffered from its effects. The leaflet explained that sometimes an addiction in a household could be recognised by the changes in the behaviour of the partner of the addict reacting to the shifts within their relationship, which made a lot of sense to me.

I was a perfectionist and still have some of those traits, but not to the same extent. My house had to be cleaned from top to bottom every week on a Monday, windows included. In my insanity, I used to think that if I started on a Sunday night, I would get ahead of myself. In our cottage we had a small solid fuel cooker that needed to be cleaned once a week so that it would not be smoking. This was the job that I hated the most, so when the stove cooled down on a Sunday night, I could take a notion to start cleaning it at maybe 10.30 pm and be outside emptying the ashes. I grew to hate ashes. There have been no open fires or stoves in the houses I lived in since.

Every week, the car had to be cleaned. I imagine my neighbour laughing if they read this since I still do clean my car every week. The grass had to be cut. Every stitch of clothes was washed and ironed. I would have argued with Robert about him going around in dirty clothes as I felt it was a reflection on me. I was so obsessed with cleanliness that I remember when our eldest child went to playschool, I would have to change my clothes going into it and then when I came back home and then back again before I collected him.

I was the type of person, even long before I got married, that always had a disagreement going on with someone. If it were not with some member of my family, it could be my boss or a workmate. I was never able to be at peace with myself and others. I was overly critical and judgemental and had high standards for myself and others. I had an opinion on what everybody around me should be doing and I didn't have a clue what I should or could be doing myself. Another thing I learned in Al-Anon was to mind my own business. I was told that if I looked inwards, I would not have the time to look outwards. This was the start of me learning not to judge myself and others.

At my first Al-Anon meeting, I exchanged my phone number with other members. In the next few days, I received phone calls from a few members of the group offering me support and guiding me to what the Al-Anon programme was all about. It was a relief to have a label for what was going on in our home and to have an explanation for an absent husband.

I thought that shouting at my husband and making idle threats would make him come home more. I was told in Al-Anon that the more I did this, the less he would come home. They were right. They asked me how I would like to be treated by my spouse if I had the disease of addiction. If he suffered from any other disease, would I treat him like this? This is where empathy came in: putting myself in his place and imagining how it felt to be him, how he could be helped and how I could make his life happier. I started to treat my husband with more respect and compassion.

One of the recovery slogans is the phrase: 'There but for the grace of God go I', which is a variation on the original phrase coined by the English preacher John Bradford (1510–1555). This is about having gratitude for help from a higher power and feeling worthy to receive it as well as having empathy with those who are suffering instead of judging them.

At that first meeting, I learned that 'gratitude changes your attitude' and that if I was grateful for what I already had, I would not see what was missing. The same goes for the people around you; if you are grateful for what they have to offer, you don't see what is missing in them. I also learned how to avoid getting into a row by thinking before I spoke and then maybe not speaking at all. 'Fake it till you make it' I was told. Learn to be an actress and don't react.

I learned to communicate better. Instead of ranting all the time, I learned to say what I mean, mean what I say and not be mean saying it. It was a case of slowing down to think before I spoke, choosing my words wisely and the tone and timing in which I delivered them. I grew stronger and more self-empowered with the help of my sponsor, who was a seasoned member of Al-Anon, guiding me through the recovery programme. Our home became peaceful because of this change in my attitude and behaviour.

I dropped my obsession with housework and started leaving the ironing board to take our children up the road or into the neighbouring fields for a walk or a ramble. I felt immense gratitude for having two healthy children, enough money, our home and a car at my door most of the time.

I continued going to my meetings twice a week and kept in touch with my recovery friends in between meetings. In the beginning, Robert did not know that I was going to the meetings as I was back home before him, but he did notice the change in me. I stopped giving out about everything and anything, so our home became a peaceful place to live, especially for our two children. I was learning how the words we choose to use and the way in which we use them can affect our lives for better or worse. People in active addiction know their family members better than they know themselves. It's all part of the disease. I let go of what was going on in my husband's life and focused on changing myself, and that was a full-time job with overtime. Dealing with addiction requires a mixture of being proactive and surrendering.

There are myriad ways to change your life for the better. What worked for me was using positive sayings, applying 'Al-Anon's Twelve Steps'[1] and saying the Serenity Prayer written by German-American theologian and Christian ethicist Reinhold Niebuhr as follows:

'God grant me the Serenity

to accept the things I cannot change,

Courage to change the things I can,

and Wisdom to know the difference.'

Before I went to Al-Anon, I had never heard of this prayer, but it is something I have come to rely on at any time of the day or in any situation, and it never lets me down. I did not know what serenity was at that time and, looking back, I didn't have it, but I gained it by inviting it into my life by changing my attitude. Serenity is what people earn in recovery, and once you get it, you will not give it up easily.

There is a little card in Al-Anon entitled 'Just for Today' with the prayer of St Francis written on the back of it. I read it every morning to understand the concept of living each day to its fullest, and this changed my attitude to life. The gratitude that had left my home then returned. My life became more manageable and meaningful. The prayer of St Francis reminds me that the purpose for us all on Earth is to be of service.

My sponsor was involved in service in Al-Anon and encouraged me to go to the area meetings with her. Service is about taking on a role to help others. It was not long before I was involved in service, too. I started by making the tea and then chairing a meeting, which was daunting the first time, but I soon got the hang of it. I went on to do a lot of service over the years, which gave me a sense of purpose and helped to build my self-esteem.

# CHAPTER TEN
# Emotional Rollercoaster

Anger and addiction are connected intricately. It was my anger that prompted me to seek help. I thought I was going mad. In recovery and through my training, I have learned that anger is a normal emotion. It lets us know that something is wrong. When you see people or children who are angry all the time, it is like a red flag to check out what is going on with that person. It is what we do with anger that makes it one letter away from danger. If we did not feel anger, we would not know when our boundaries were crossed or, when we crossed those of other people or when we crossed our own boundaries. Underneath the emotion of anger there can be a lot of feelings such as fear, shame, guilt, isolation or loneliness, etc. Anger can also be the strongest emotion experienced following a traumatic event and is one of the five stages of grief.

Resentment is like swallowing the poison and hoping it will kill someone else. It is like re-sensing or feeling again the negative emotions. It is one thing to feel anger initially, but it is another thing to replay a negative scene or conversation in your mind, dredging up the hurt and anger again and again. Resentments are something you cannot afford in recovery. They are the number one relapse trigger. Underneath most relapses, there lies a resentment. In recovery, we learn to deal with our resentments. We are told that if we want to get rid of our resentments, we need to be willing to let them go. We are invited to pray for the person or people we resent and ask our higher power to help us remove our resentments.

During group work on releasing resentments, I often ask the participants if I could wave a magic wand and remove all their resentments. How would they feel? The answer is always the same: lighter, free and happy. We all have a choice whether to hold on to resentment or not.

Shame and guilt are powerful emotions. We are not born with them. They are emotions that we experience along life's journey. They are associated with wrongdoing. These two emotions are self-conscience emotions in that they promote good or bad behaviour. We experience these emotions in the context of other people. Most people who are living in a place of shame don't know it. These emotions can have a major impact on our lives. Guilt creates a feeling of having done something wrong and a realisation about having made a mistake. Guilt is a more positive emotion than shame because it sends a message to change and make amends. It motivates a person to address the problem. It prompts people to apologise or confess.

Shame does not promote change. Shame brings up all sorts of negative thoughts such as 'I'm the black sheep of the family', 'I was told I would never amount to anything', 'I was told I was stupid at school – the teacher made a show of me' or 'If you really knew me you wouldn't like me', etc. Unfortunately, most people with an addiction – and their family members – carry shame for their addiction or their family member's addiction. They feel that somehow they are responsible for having an addiction, that they choose this illness. Before recovery, family members often feel they are to blame for the other person's addiction, and due to the nature of addiction, they are often blamed by the addicted person and society in general. Intense feelings of shame result in self-defeating behaviours such as social withdrawal or isolation, addictive and compulsive behaviours such as eating, drinking, drug-taking and gambling, etc.

No other illness – except possibly HIV – carries the stigma and shame that addiction does. It is a hindrance to people seeking help and recovery. I always ask people if they had any other illness, would they feel ashamed of it, and the answer is always 'no'. So, we need to change our attitude to the suffering caused by addiction. The good news is that feelings of shame can be changed. Since shame is a learned emotion or behaviour, it can be unlearned and replaced by more positive attitudes, behaviours and feelings. We can lessen the feelings of shame by understanding its roots, acknowledging that we feel shame and changing our shame-related behaviours. Author Brené Brown says: 'Shame is the birthplace of perfectionism.'[6]

# CHAPTER ELEVEN
# A Question of Trust

I was not that long in Al-Anon when my sponsor suggested that I not be surprised if there was more than work going on in my husband's life due to the time he spent out of our home. I trusted him to the end of the Earth and never questioned where he was or what he was doing. A short time later, this person's suspicions were confirmed. I would have always said that I would not put up with certain types of behaviour, but you never really know how you will react to a situation until you are in it.

I was so lucky that I was in Al-Anon at that time and had plenty of support and understanding, as the old me would have reacted a whole different way. I accepted his behaviour at the time as a side effect of addiction, which it was, as there is often more than one problem associated with one person's addiction. I was not well enough at that time to deal with it, so I continued to work on myself, being aware that if his behaviour continued, I would have to address it later. I mentioned to my husband the rumours I had heard, but he told me that it was not true. I started asking questions as to his whereabouts for the first time in my life.

People in active addiction are incapable of telling the truth as they try to hide or protect their addiction. Addiction is a disease in which you tell yourself you don't have it. Denial is part of the disease for both family members and the person suffering from the disease. Going into recovery is like being in a dense fog, and as you begin to recover, the fog begins to lift, and you start to see life more clearly.

I kept attending my meetings and eventually established a boundary that if my husband's behaviour outside the home continued, I was not going to continue to live with it. When this boundary was crossed several times, I went to a solicitor and then to court for a legal separation. His drinking had got worse since it was a progressive disease. Soon after our separation, my husband decided to go into an addiction treatment unit to deal with his addiction, and this filled me with hope that he would change and recover so we could get our life together back. I had seen a married couple who were both in recovery speak at a convention a few months before this. The wife was in Al-Anon, and her husband was in Alcoholics Anonymous. I thought that this could be my husband and I in the future.

I was asked to go to the addiction unit for a joint interview, which was not helpful to either of us. I visited my husband on visiting days with our children. Robert was not happy there, and on his last weekend of the treatment programme, when he was allowed to go home, he relapsed, and that ended the treatment. Treatment centres differ, and in those days, a lot of them employed shame-based practices. They tried to break the person into submission rather than using compassion, empathy and education.

Author Terence Real said: 'An addict needs shame like a man dying of thirst needs salt water.'[7] Society needs to change the way it deals with addiction. People need to change the way they approach and talk about addiction to encourage addicts to seek help along with their families, who often isolate in shame. This can happen when their loved one gets into trouble as a result of their altered behaviour through their addiction, and the story may be printed in the local newspapers.

After the relapse, we were offered counselling, which we both attended. I think Robert was going to some AA meetings, too. When my husband came to see the children, he led me to believe that all he wanted was to come back home. I remember going to speak to a wise member of Al-Anon to see what I should do, and she encouraged me to take him back, so I did.

But it wasn't long until the old familiar pattern began to repeat itself, so we returned to counselling and marriage guidance sessions. But I felt hopeless as the bottom line in any relationship is that as much as you love someone, you cannot change anyone else unless they want to change, especially when there is an addiction involved. The addiction was like a squatter in my marriage. I wanted it arrested once and for all, but I didn't have that authority, and Robert appeared to be unable to commit to the recovery programme. This unwelcome guest seemed to be stronger than both of us. We struggled for another six to eight months until I set a boundary of what was acceptable to me going forward, and I made it clear that if it were crossed again, our marriage would be over.

At that time, even with all the Al-Anon recovery I had undertaken, separation from Robert was not what I wanted, but accepting Robert's unacceptable behaviour was taking a toll on me. My boundary was crossed a couple more times, and, in my confusion as to what to do, I spoke to a priest about my situation and the suggestion he gave me was, 'You must do what is right for you'. It felt like God himself had spoken to me. I knew that if I continued to live the way I was living, I may not be around long enough to rear our children.

When I saw Robert a few days later, I told him that our marriage was over. Dealing with addiction requires tough love, and if I was willing to accept unacceptable behaviour, I was enabling his addiction by making the situation too comfortable for him to want to change anything. I knew that by continuing to live the way we were, I was showing our children that this was a normal way to live, and I didn't want that.

When you make the decision to separate from your husband, I believe your title changes from being a 'fool' for putting up with the unacceptable behaviour to being a 'bitch' for establishing reasonable boundaries. One of the reasons I stayed in the marriage as long as I did was probably because I never wanted the stigma and shame associated with separation. Before I went through a separation, I would have judged other couples who had gone through this, never realising the pain they had to deal with in splitting up. My separation from Robert humbled me. I lost any notion that I was better than anyone else. I stopped judging myself and others. I began to look upon separated couples through the eye of compassion. I was reminded that nobody is perfect, including myself. Sometimes, we can put too high expectations upon ourselves and others, which can lead to disappointment. This came partly from the perfectionist in me. My pride took a blow, and I learned how to ask for help. I was given support by some good neighbours, friends, family and Al-Anon Family Groups members. I was starting to view myself, my family and my world differently, like I had zoomed out from my life to see the bigger picture. This higher perspective enabled me to see the consequences of choices and the workings of cause and effect.

# CHAPTER TWELVE
# The Caretaker

Examining my behaviour and my husband's and the effect we were having on our children made me reflect on my own childhood, and it brought questions to my mind. How had I become like this? How had I ended up in a situation like this? What factors had produced this environment? My eyes were opened to see we had transitioned into a dysfunctional relationship.

Catherine Winter wrote an article on the website 'A Conscious Rethink', which identifies twelve dysfunctional family roles[8] as follows: 1. The narcissist (or borderline); 2. The addict; 3. The co-dependent (enabler); 4. The caretaker; 5. The golden child (hero); 6. The rebel (defender); 7. The waif; 8. The black sheep/scapegoat; 9. The clown; 10. The peacemaker; 11. The lost child; and 12. The manipulator or mastermind.

It is worth reading about the traits of each of these roles to see which ones, if any, you may identify with for yourself, the addict and your family members. If any of these roles apply to the family members that someone in recovery grew up with or is living with now, they can learn to see how behaviours and patterns in themselves and the people around them may have influenced their journey with addiction and recovery.

I can identify myself as 'the little caretaker', who – as a result of their own anxiety – has a tendency to spend their time focusing on helping others to feel better. They can be motherly in their relationships with other children or with a parent. They gain validation by approval for taking responsibility. They often grow up to become a partner of an addicted person if they do not get help. I read once that feeling that you are loved for what you do and not for who you are describing a 'caretaker'.

Many people in the caring profession are the 'caretaker'. Most partners of people in addiction are 'caretakers' too, and in doing lectures in treatment centres, it is surprising how many people in addiction also identify as caretakers from their own childhood. It is a lovely trait to have, except when you caretake at the expense of yourself. Then, it turns into a defect of character. It is all about finding balance.

Codependency can be common in relationships with people in addiction. It can occur between a parent and child or between partners or with friends.

Author Melody Beattie said: 'A co-dependent person is one who has let another person's behaviour affect him or her, and who is obsessed with controlling that person's behaviour'.[9]

A simple way of describing a codependent relationship is when your happiness depends on the feelings of another person. If they are happy, you are happy. If they are sad, you are sad. This can also occur in any needy relationship. In recovery, it is possible to be happy regardless of what another person is feeling, no matter how closely you are connected with them.

# CHAPTER THIRTEEN
## Going it Alone

The transition from being part of a couple to being a single mother takes time. All I saw were happy families everywhere. Just like when a woman longs to have a child, she sees children and pregnant women all around her. This just goes to show how powerful our thoughts are at creating the reality around us.

Saying 'I' instead of 'we' reminded me I was on my own. Something else that also became apparent to me is how we exist in a couple-oriented society. When you are in a couple, you are invited to join other couples for social events, but when you are on your own, you are often overlooked. Couples seem to forget what it is like for single people to attend weddings, funerals or social events on their own, often feeling like a spare part or not having someone familiar to talk to, sit with or dance with. I often felt like the odd one out after my separation from Robert. I had to adjust my mind and lifestyle to this. Over time, I gained more courage, self-confidence and independence. Today, I can happily go anywhere on my own with my higher power by my side. I was brave enough to go for a week's holiday to Spain on my own about 14 years ago and had a nice, quiet, peaceful time getting much-needed rest from my busy work schedule at home. I had no one to answer to but myself and could set my own itinerary to suit me.

When someone tells me they are worried about what other people think, I ask them: 'Are these people that you are worried about doing anything for you, or are they going to pay your bills? If the answer is 'no' then I wouldn't worry what they think.' I am not so important that people would worry about what I am doing or where I am going, but if I stay in the house and do nothing then I am the one who will miss out on life.

When you are single or a single parent, there is an illusion held by people in general that you are the one who has the most time on your hands to help others and that you have the resources to do so. But being a single parent doubles your workload along with living on a single income. There is no bed of roses on either side of the fence. This is not something anyone would choose if they had a better option.

There was a difficult and emotional transition period for acceptance of our new situation. As the American community activist and political theorist Saul Alinsky said: 'Change means movement. Movement means friction.'[10]

Separation in a marriage seems to spark feelings of shame in the extended family, who prefer not to mention it. But because they don't like to talk about it, they often don't know the full story and could lay blame where it doesn't belong. I was so grateful to have the support of my friends in Al-Anon, as some of them had been through a similar experience and were able to guide me on how to deal with it. When a spouse dies, people automatically offer the surviving spouse sympathy, respect and support, but when you get separated, you have to earn other people's respect.

Robert continued to see our children regularly and supported their upbringing, and he still does so to this day. Our children know they are loved and supported by both of us and in any difficulty, we work together as a family unit. A year or so after our separation, my husband met a new partner, and they set up a home together. I am happy for them both.

Being a single parent brought me financial instability. Our youngest child had not started school by then, so when September came, and I was complaining to my sponsor about the lack of money, she told me to look at the job adverts in the newspaper. I applied for three jobs and got one in the kitchen of a local secondary school. It took a lot of courage to go to work in the local village. Sometime later, I saw an advert for a job offering better hours in the primary school with an Enterprise Ulster Scheme attached to it to encourage people to go back to work full-time. My application was successful.

# CHAPTER FOURTEEN
## Self-realisation

To be accepted on the Enterprise Ulster Scheme I had to be interviewed by a man called Melvin Scofield. He asked me about my work history, and I replied shamefully, 'I just worked in a shop for ten years'. He wanted to know exactly what I had done in all that time. I explained that I had done everything from stock control to the window displays to training new staff and that I was able to step into any department and run it effectively when there were other staff off. I was also particularly good at customer service. I had never felt good enough because I didn't do my exams. However, throughout this interview, as I assessed my previous job, I gained a new perspective on and appreciation of the skills and talents that it took to be a good and valued shop assistant. I had dealt with people on a daily basis in the shop, but until that moment I had never taken stock of what great skills I had acquired and used efficiently.

A talent is something you can do easily that others would find difficult. We are all multi-talented individuals, but sadly, most of us do not know or own our own talents. A therapist once described people in addiction as 'multi-talented people with no self-worth'. I think the same can be said for their partners. Today, I own every talent that I have, and there are others I still have to discover. It is said that when we reach the gates of heaven, we should have no talents left to discover because we have used them all.

I was accepted onto the Enterprise Ulster Scheme, which included doing several short certified courses at the end of which we were given a folder with all our achievements listed in it. I thought it was a CV, but later discovered it was nothing like a CV, but seeing all my achievements on paper gave me a confidence boost.

Now that I had a good job, I decided to investigate if I would be eligible to get a grant to help me renovate the cottage, as it only had two bedrooms and no central heating. I was advised by an excellent builder in our area how to go about this. I qualified for a part grant to renovate our home, but I had to come up with the rest of the money. I had a sharp reminder of my circumstances of being a single parent and a woman when I went to the bank for a loan. I will not go into detail, but I am sure no man had to go through the hoops that I had to. Thanks to assistance from my sister and her husband, I was able to get enough money to start the work on my house.

I am sure the builder would agree with me when I say that I did not have a clue about anything to do with renovations, but I learned along the way. It took over a year to complete the renovations, and I had a lovely new home to move back into, far beyond my expectations. When it was almost completed, I knew I did not have enough money to get it painted inside, but I was relieved to have the main work done.

Out of the blue I received a call from a relative of mine to say that herself and another relative were coming to visit me. I found this peculiar since it was usually my mother that they went to see. We had a nice time during their visit, and before they left the one who had called me gave me an envelope with enough money in it to get the inside of my house painted. I could write a book solely about many moments like this that happened to me when I least expected it. I call these 'higher power moments'.

Moving back into the cottage filled me with much joy, but I was also awash with sadness as this was the dream that Robert and I had shared when we got to the cottage. I would have never thought that I would be able to do this project on my own, and I had never imagined it would be that way. It probably took me another ten years to get it half-middling, but it was my first big achievement while working on the 'Al-Anon Twelve Steps'[1] programme. I prayed about every part

52

of it and took it one day at a time throughout the whole project while working hard to pay back my loans. It was then that I felt that I earned respect among my community and family.

During these years, my confidence grew through doing the basic courses with Enterprise Ulster and from doing varied service in Al-Anon. People were drawn to me to get support in changing their lives. My children could testify that their mammy was on the phone a lot during the evenings, giving suggestions and support to others in need.

This inspired me to go to college to undertake a basic counselling course to be in a better position to help other people while gaining some personal development. I had no aspiration to become a therapist as I believed that was above my intellect. I loved the proud and content feeling while walking around the college even though I had no belief in myself. From that first course in 1998, I went on to complete several more courses and training in counselling and learning support, and bereavement and loss, to training and volunteering with a local listening ear service and then training as a facilitator with Accord to facilitate pre-marriage courses. I facilitated with Accord for three years and enjoyed this immensely. To this day, I have a passion for facilitating groups.

# CHAPTER FIFTEEN
# Employment Endeavours

I had always said that as soon as my children were old enough and had left school, I would go back to work full-time. Being at home when our children came home from school was something I felt strongly about, as it was how I was reared. When I got home from school, my mother had my dinner ready, and I wanted to do this for my children.

When thinking about getting a full-time job, I sought the help of an organisation called Obair, which assisted people with many initiatives, including employability. I connected with a supportive staff member called Melissa, who helped me compile my CV and fill out a few application forms. I was offered two jobs and accepted one of them as a fitness technician in a new ladies' fitness centre called Curves that was soon to open in Monaghan Town.

Within a few weeks of being in this job, the manager's position became available and I put myself forward for it and got it. I had a lot of learning to do on the job, including working on a computer, learning to operate the fitness machines and managing and training other staff members. This was a job that I loved as it had a great ethos to support women's fitness and the local community.

As it was a franchise business it also encouraged women to own their own business. This was a great experience for me, along with getting a chance to go to London to a conference where I met the founder of Curves, Gary Heavin. I met so many lovely women in this job, and under my management, the membership was one of the highest of the ten centres.

During this time, I developed an idea for a business of my own. I had already completed a course on starting your own business, so I took a risk and tried it out. It lasted about four weeks, and I discovered that I did not like it when I got a chance to do it. I still think my business idea is a good one, but it's more suited to a city with a bigger population. I was lucky that I had not given up my full-time job to try this enterprise. I settled myself and felt gratitude for my full-time job. I was glad that I had got this business idea out of my head to free my mind to explore other opportunities.

I saw an advertisement in my local newspaper looking to employ someone who loved house cleaning and wanted to own their own business. I got a friend of mine to check the company out to discover it was a franchise business that was for sale. I made an appointment to meet the owner.

From the moment I met the owner, we hit it off, and I was interested in buying this business. I now had the experience of managing a franchise business and was an excellent cleaner, so all I had to do was raise the money to purchase it. I travelled to England to undertake some training with another franchise operator and also received training at the franchise base from the owner. My local Credit Union gave me the loan I needed to purchase the business, and in January 2005, I became the proud owner of my own cleaning business.

I employed a woman to work for me in the business, and we have been good friends since then. We worked extremely hard but also had great fun along the way. On busy days, I employed casual workers to help complete the big contracts. In 2007, I was featured in 'Franchise Magazine' along with the other franchise owners in the area, highlighting the success of our businesses.

I was contracted to keep the cleaning business for five years, but before I had it for three years, I met someone who told me about an international counselling course that focused on addiction. It was delivered in Co. Tipperary, and in addition to studying, each student had to find a placement in a treatment centre to gain practical experience. It sounded like the type of course that I would love to do, but it was not easy to get a place on it, and, like most courses, it was not cheap. I owned my business and had it at full capacity. I could have expanded it, but I always knew that this business was a stepping stone for me to something less strenuous. I had just read Rhonda Byrne's book *'The Secret'* [11], which is based on the law of attraction, meaning what you think about a lot – whether good or bad - or focusing on what you fear is what you will attract into your life. So, if you want to achieve something positive, then you need to focus your thoughts on it and take action in that direction. So, I applied for the course and used the law of attraction to manifest an invitation to attend an interview in Tipperary at the end of January. This lightened up the cold, dark wintry days. But when the snowdrops and daffodils peeped their heads as April approached, I still had not heard anything. I knew that I would need to have my cleaning business sold by August if I was going to be able to join the course in October. Everything seemed to be up in the air, like a feather twirling about on a breeze, not knowing which terrain or pathway it was going to land upon. I didn't like feeling adrift, so I decided to take action and put my business up for sale after speaking to the franchiser. He was always aware of my passion for counselling work and kindly supported me in pursuing this. To this day, we are still good friends.

A few weeks later, I got a letter to say I had been accepted to the counselling course and by the end of August, my business was sold. I felt like I was working with the law of attraction, and it was working with and for me. I had to travel to a few treatment centres around Ireland to secure a placement. I was accepted in a few of them but chose one in Co. Wexford called Aiseiri. There was something special about this place and the people in it that attracted me.

I started my training, and life became hectic. Four-and-a-half hours of driving each way at the weekends, then cleaning my house, cutting the grass, doing my washing and ironing, and all the usual visits made life busy. But I remained focused on my goal during my training. I look back on that time and wonder how I got through it. Somehow, when your heart and mind yearn for something, you find the courage, energy and resources to pursue and achieve it. My health was not great towards the end of the training as my blood count was extremely low, which took a toll on my energy. Somehow, with the help of my higher power, I got through it.

I was incredibly lucky with my accommodation in Wexford, which I found through my brother's best man. He worked with a man who had a holiday home outside Wexford, which was ideal for me. It was in a small village that had a shop and a chapel. It was my home from home that allowed me to study without distractions.

When I was in Tipperary, we all had to stay in the same accommodation where the training took place, and we would be studying up to 10.00 pm some nights. It was very intense but enjoyable. There was never a day that I ever regretted my decision to go on this adventure. It was a costly time, too, but thanks to the support of people close to me and the money I gained from selling my business, I got through. I am grateful to all the people who supported me in myriad ways to get me qualified in counselling because, without them, I would not have been able to help all the people that I have assisted. As the saying goes, 'it takes a village'.

Having dyslexia, I thought I would struggle with keeping up with the rest of the class. Being a perfectionist helped me to persist in doing the best I could, along with being determined and self-disciplined. I made great friends in Wexford and they will always hold a special place in my heart for the encouragement they gave me. I went to my Al-Anon meetings both in Tipperary and in Wexford and made friends there too. They reminded me to take it one day at a time and trust in my higher power that I would succeed, as there was no backup plan.

My sister, her husband, my mother and my two children, along with one of my dearest friends, made the long trip to Tipperary to attend my graduation in October 2009. It was one of the happiest days of my life. The staff lit a candle for the people who couldn't make it, so in my graduation speech, I recalled my younger sister, who passed away in 2001 from cancer. I am sure she was up there in heaven saying at last, I realised that I could do more with my life as she had often encouraged me to do some courses, but at that time, I dismissed it as I thought I wasn't capable of doing anything like that. It was fantastic to have finished my studies, but now I had to look for a job.

# CHAPTER SIXTEEN
# Home Help

I had made some contacts in treatment centres when I was looking for a placement for the counselling course. After I graduated, I got in touch with them to see if they had any work available. Out of the blue, I got a call from a woman in Derry/Londonderry to say that there was a vacancy for a counsellor in a new project that was funded for three years, and she encouraged me to apply for it.

An Al-Anon friend accompanied me to Derry/Londonderry. I had only been there once before and didn't know my way around. It is quite a small city when you get to know it, but it felt like an overwhelming maze to me then. So, my friend helped to quell my nerves as together we located the venue where my interview was taking place. I had gained so much independence over the years, but obtaining this post was so important to me that I felt like I needed someone to lean on.

On graduating, I was told that to get my accreditation, I had to work in the field for at least three years to gain all my supervision hours along with my own personal therapy hours. The post in Derry/Londonderry would provide me with the opportunity to fulfil this criteria. There was an oratory in the building and I was asked to wait in it. In those peaceful surroundings, I prayed to my higher power that I would get the job. My response was interrupted when I was called into the interview. My nerves started to kick in, and I hoped my interviewer would not feel the clamminess building on my palms when we shook hands. Because this post seemed vital to me, I wasn't as natural in the interview as I would have liked to have been, but I felt that I performed satisfactorily.

I was ecstatic when I was asked to start the role on 3$^{rd}$ January 2010. But the weather had other plans. That winter was known as 'The Big Freeze of 2010' as it was the coldest winter recorded since 1987. The extreme weather meant I did not get a chance to go up to Derry/Londonderry to secure accommodation before my start date. I left home on 2$^{nd}$ January with my car packed with everything that I might need, looking for somewhere to stay with little time to spare. It reminded me of Mary and Joseph setting off on a loaded donkey to find a room at the inn with the clock ticking before the big event. I had made an appointment with an estate agent to show me some flats at 2.00 pm. The journey to Derry/Londonderry was slow and treacherous, with heavy snow and ice on the roads, and the car window wipers were freezing all the way. It seemed that even the elements were testing my resolve.

I never felt so relieved to arrive somewhere as when I got to Derry/Londonderry that day. I parked in a car park, gained my composure after the tense drive and took a taxi to the estate agent. He drove me around the city centre, showing me some flats that were dire. I asked him if these were the best that he had for the money I was willing to pay, and he said 'yes'. I told him that if I had to live in any of those flats, I would not survive. He assured me that I would not find what I was looking for. Deflated, I parted company with him and got directions back to my car. On the way back, I called another few estate agents with no luck. I had an Al-Anon friend who lived in Strabane who had told me that if I were stuck for a place to stay, I could reside with her until I found somewhere. I phoned her, but there was no answer, so I left her a message.

Before I reached my car, I realised I was not far from the oratory I had prayed in before my interview, so I decided to go there to say a prayer to find the right accommodation. God knows I needed some help. Just before I reached the oratory, I passed another estate agency and decided to go into it. I was greeted by a young man working there and asked him if there were any small flats to rent. He asked me when I needed it, and I replied 'today'. With that, he put on his coat and instructed, 'follow me'. We walked around the corner and a little way up the street, where he brought me into a building site of an old Georgian house that was being converted into flats. One of the flats was closer to completion than the rest. He explained that this flat should be ready before the end of the week. It was exactly what I wanted. It was brand new, the price was right, and it was in the perfect location. It was beside my workplace and a five-minute walk from Guildhall Square with on-street parking, something that I had not considered before.

My friend in Strabane phoned me back, and I went to stay with her for a few nights until I got the keys to what was to be my home for the next three years. I loved Derry/Londonderry City. My morning walk took me over the Craigavon Bridge and then the Peace Bridge when it opened. I was there in 2013 when Derry/Londonderry was the UK's first 'City of Culture'. I lived five minutes' walk from Guildhall Square on 15th June 2010 when the then Prime Minister David Cameron's apology for the Bloody Sunday killings of 1972 was broadcast from the House of Commons onto large screens in the square. The world was changing, as was my inner world. The landscape was morphing into something new for me to explore. I was in Derry/Londonderry for the heavy snowfall of winter 2010-11 when temperatures plummeted, causing the coldest December since Met Office records commenced. The roads were practically impassable, and I still remember the hairy drive home that Christmas. I met a lot of lovely people in Derry/Londonderry, some of whom have become dear friends that I meet up with when I go back for a day trip to my favourite city. I attended an Al-Anon meeting on a Tuesday evening in Letterkenny weekly and it felt like a home from home.

I settled well into my new job and it took time to build up the project. Part of my role as a counsellor and facilitator was to deliver an education and family programme on addiction. I developed a programme like that during my training, so I just had to update it and add a few more pieces to it. I started delivering the one-day and sometimes two-day programme in Derry/Londonderry on a regular basis. I loved having the opportunity to help families of people suffering from a loved one's addiction. I was invited to speak on a few radio stations advertising this programme along with being interviewed by the local newspapers.

In my third year in Derry/Londonderry, I saw an advertisement from Nexus NI (an organisation that counsels adult survivors of sexual abuse) looking for counsellors to do a placement with them and avail of their training and supervision. This was not something that I had ever envisaged myself doing, but since sexual abuse came up so much in my work with people with addictions, I thought I would apply for the placement. I was called for the interview, part of which involved a role play, and I was successful. I worked there one evening per week after the initial training. This was a great but challenging experience for me, pushing me out of my comfort zone.

Towards the end of my three years in Derry/Londonderry, there appeared to be little desire to keep the project running and no funding available to do so. Sadly, I knew that if this project ended, there would be many people who would miss the service we had provided.

I was feeling very tired at this time. The uncertainty of what I was going to do when I went back home to continue my counselling career was daunting. I was unable to save money due to the outgoings of renting my flat and maintaining my cottage. I had applied for my accreditation at the end of my three years and was waiting for the response. I arrived home that December to find the accreditation acceptance letter waiting for me in the post. My heart began to race, and I thought how strange it was that a small piece of paper could arouse so many emotions of anticipation, excitement and fear. My shaking fingers opened the envelope nervously, and I was delighted to discover I was now fully qualified. I was offered some part-time work with the project up to about April, which included facilitating my education and family programme and one-to-one counselling.

# CHAPTER SEVENTEEN
## Unexpected News

Around March 2013, I visited my GP for a routine appointment. I mentioned to him that after walking up the stairs or a hill, I felt out of breath. The doctor listened to my breathing. I was sent for a chest X-ray, which revealed an abnormality. I was asked to attend a clinic at the hospital, where the consultant told me he needed to perform a biopsy to determine what was wrong with me. Worrying about the results made me feel more tired than I had been, and my anxiety was prolonged because my GP was away on holiday when I phoned to obtain my results. The wait felt like forever.

On his return, my doctor informed me that I had a rare condition known as pulmonary sarcoidosis in my lungs. I had not heard of this disease, for which there is no known certain cause or cure. I was pleased to learn it may go away on its own and devastated that it can last for months or years and may need to be managed with steroids. It causes fatigue, pain and swelling in the joints, and when it affects the lungs, it can bring on a persistent dry cough, wheezing or chest pain. The condition causes small clusters of cells, known as granulomas, to develop in organs of the body. While my lungs were affected, it can also affect the lymph nodes, eyes, heart, skin and other organs and appear as swollen tissue. It is an autoimmune disease that usually begins in people aged between 30 and 40 and affects more women than men. It may be triggered by environmental factors such as a reaction to chemicals, dust, infectious material or an abnormal reaction to the body's own proteins in a person who may be predisposed genetically to it. From now on, I was to have regular check-ups in the hospital with my consultant. I didn't know what had caused it – genetics or the environment or both – but it did cross my mind that it could have been triggered by all the chemicals I had used for years when cleaning my home fastidiously and in my cleaning business.

The summer that I was diagnosed, the weather was lovely. Since I had little energy, work or money, I decided to rest and relax outdoors while getting a suntan, not knowing that the sun and sarcoidosis do not mix. I found out that I need to wear sunscreen with factor 50 if I am exposed to the sun as not only did it drain the little energy I had left, but an overproduction of Vitamin D from sunlight can cause the level of calcium in the body of a person with sarcoidosis to become too high. I also had to cut down on my consumption of dairy products because of this.

I am lucky that in my local town, there was a support group for people suffering from sarcoidosis. A facilitator in the group called Wendy Watson organised guest speakers, Dr McManus and Professor Donnelly, who came from Dublin once a year, from whom I learned a great deal about the condition. I was told that sarcoidosis could take 10 years off my life due to the constant wear and tear on my lungs. This unwelcome revelation made it feel like a part of my life that I had been looking forward to – part of my future that I had taken for granted – was suddenly being stolen from me. Because of this, I have become incredibly good at time management and self-care. If I know I have a busy day ahead, I plan to rest the next day.

It's hard to describe what it is like when you haven't the energy to stop at the shop on your way home from work, or if you invite visitors when you have energy and then on the day they are due to come you hardly have the energy to talk to them and hope they don't stay too late. I don't want to see or hear from anybody after 10.00 pm as that is my bedtime. Eight years after my diagnosis, I still have sarcoidosis, and sometimes it flares up badly. When I have energy, I tend to do too much, which I pay for later with exhaustion.

When people ask me about my social life, I tell them that it is non-existent except for the cinema, lunch or early evening meals out. I used to love going out dancing and could have been on the dance floor from the first dance to the last, but now I go dancing maybe once a year, and a couple of dances are enough. Exercising with sarcoidosis is like kindling its fire. I would have to be sure I had little to do for a few days after a night out.

Despite my diagnosis and lack of energy, I enjoyed being back at home after several busy years away with hardly any time off to relax. I linked in with a programme that supported people to become self-employed to help me start my own counselling business. I set up my website with the help of my cousin, got my business cards printed and made a few phone calls. I was lucky to get some sessional hours with Nexus NI as I had worked with them in Derry/Londonderry and to get the chance to develop and facilitate the Time Out Programme in Action Mental Health along with doing one-to-one support there, too. I talked to one of the service users about facilitating a women's group there, so she approached the manager, who liked the idea and gave it to go-ahead. Sadly, this woman is no longer with us. This was a great group of women supporting each other to change and grow, and we also had great fun. This programme was so successful that it was funded for an extra year.

I was then invited to facilitate the Journey Together Group in the Aisling Centre in Enniskillen, Co. Fermanagh, which supported family members who were affected by a loved one's addiction. I also did outreach work for them along with one-to-one sessional counselling in the centre. I facilitated my own accredited Education Programme on Addiction and my second one-day programme on Feelings and Emotions Associated with Addiction. I was happy and content with the variety of work I had and the lovely people I met through it. While some people with sarcoidosis are unable to work, I am still able to, for which I am deeply grateful since I love my work so much.

# CHAPTER EIGHTEEN
## Moving On

At this stage in my life, our children had moved on with their lives, and I was living alone and working full time while spending my spare time in a pair of wellington boots outside, either cutting or strimming the grass, spraying the weeds with a back sprayer, cutting the hedge or painting the fence. I reflected on some of my absurd behaviour in the past. I remember telling a young couple about my crazy behaviour before I found Al-Anon when I had no hedge clippers or strimmer to cut the grass underneath the fence, so I cut the grass with a pair of scissors. The woman I told this to replied that she had done the same thing. There are a lot of 'me too's' when you live with addiction.

As I was getting older and with the long drive to work, I often thought of moving closer to Enniskillen, but this was something that I never really thought I would have the courage to do. I had put so much effort and time into improving the cottage, but living away from home for a few years showed me that I could be content anywhere if I have my higher power with me and have peace of mind. I also felt a sense of loyalty to the people in my home neighbourhood. Then, one day, someone said something to me that freed my mind. After discussing what this person said and the potential move with my friend, I made up my mind that I was going to put my house up for sale. Looking back, I realise that person was the messenger my higher power sent me to make a move, and I am grateful for that person.

I made up my mind to tell my ex-husband and our children of my plans the next time I saw them. One evening, a short time later, I was sitting watching TV when in walked one of my children with my ex-husband on their way home from somewhere. This was a 'higher power moment' as this was not something that usually happened. I told them about my plans as I really was not fit to continue all the manual labour that it took for the upkeep of the cottage and garden. Neither of our children had the time to do any of it. They said that, ultimately, it was up to me what to do, but they were concerned that I would not like living in a town.

I put the cottage up for sale, and, as in country areas, it was the talk of the countryside for a while. I felt hurt when I heard some of the gossip about the speculations about my reasons for selling. I had never sold a house before and knew nothing about the process. I learned about the different estate agents and the way they work. I learned to be patient in the process and, in the end, thought that my higher power must have meant for me to stay where I was.

I kept the cottage on the market but decided to replace the bathroom, which was a renovation I had hoped someone else would be doing. In December, halfway through the revamp of the bathroom, I got a viewing. That week, I received an offer on my house, and I accepted it. I then needed somewhere to live and had been looking in an area that I thought I would like to live in. There was a house for sale there that needed quite a bit of work done to it, starting with the fence. The same estate agent who was selling my house was selling this one, and he was a gentleman. I went to view the house twice and brought a friend to see it once and put an offer on it, which was accepted.

One of Louise L. Hay's affirmations at the end of her book *'You Can Heal Your Life'* [12] was: 'My house will sell quickly and easily, the move will be easy to do, I will love my new home and my neighbours'. I kept repeating this affirmation after I put my cottage up for sale, and I can honestly say this was how it happened. I sold and bought a house in one day and slept in my new house that night. I have not looked back since.

# CHAPTER NINETEEN
# Words for Change

Phrases and sayings that can be repeated frequently are often the first tools that a person entering into recovery uses to make the first changes in their day-to-day living.

Repeating 'just for today' was one of the first recovery tools that I held on to. Living one day at a time had been foreign to me. I was always trying to get ahead of myself, such as with my over-the-top cleaning routine that began on a Sunday evening. Looking into the past too often kept me wallowing in self-pity, and I lost many a day living in the present as a result.

Telling myself 'easy does it' and 'first things first' and asking myself 'how important is it?' reminded me to slow down, to do one thing at a time and not to struggle to try to do several things at once. These words helped me to let go of things and stop worrying about what other people said.

There is a saying in the recovery rooms to 'keep an open mind' and keep things simple and this will enable you to find help. Closed-minded people find recovery hard, if not impossible. Recovery is a simple programme for complicated people. The more educated a person is when they enter the recovery rooms, the more difficult they can find it to grasp that such a simple programme can work miracles in their life.

'Let go and let God' is a powerful phrase to help a person's mind overcome being tormented by fear and anxiety. Repeating this slogan took whatever I was obsessing about out of my thoughts.

I learned a poem written by Erwin Lutzer about letting go and letting God, as follows:

'As children bring their broken toys

with tears for us to mend,

I brought my broken dreams to God.

because He was my friend, and then,

instead of letting go, I hung around.

and tried to help in ways that were my own,

at last, I snatched them back and cried.

"How can You be so slow?"

My Child, He said, "What could I do, you never did let go!"[13]

In one of the readings at Al-Anon, a woman spoke about putting the slogan 'let go and let God' into action by getting herself a box, which she called her 'God box'. Whenever she had a problem, she took a pen and paper and wrote a letter to God and put it into the box and put the lid on it. Whenever she thought about the problem, she said to herself, 'God has it', which gave her contentment to get on with her day. I have a God box, as do a lot of people who heard me tell this story and it really works. Once I write down whatever it is that is causing me concern, which is not often, it takes whatever it is out of my head. It is all about how much we trust.

'Listen and learn' reminds me that I have two ears and one mouth, so I should listen twice as much as I speak. Some people say that we should take the cotton wool out of our ears and put it in our mouths. Need I say more!

'Let it begin with me' encouraged me to get involved in service in Al-Anon, which was a big part of my recovery as it encouraged me to read a lot to understand the service part of the programme, and, of course, being a perfectionist encouraged that too. If you are inclined to stand back and let other people take the lead, this phrase challenges a person to change that.

'Live and let live' – to 'live' was a big challenge for me and a lot of people in early recovery as it encourages people to live rather than exist. I did not have a clue how to live. I rarely went anywhere, did anything or tried anything new. If there was something that I would have liked to go to, instead of trying to get there, I would have avoided it and felt relieved when it was over and then it went out of my mind. During recovery, I tried to go to new places and do new things such as going to a concert and the cinema or on holiday, etc. Instead of letting life pass me by, I started taking an active part in my life. 'Let live' was easier when I started to focus on myself and mind my own business.

'One day at a time'[14] is the essence of the whole recovery programme. For people in early recovery, the message is simple: if you can stay away from whatever your addiction is just for today, then you can do the same tomorrow. For family members, it is the same message: if they can get through today, they will get through tomorrow.

'This too shall pass' means that everything changes. Nothing stays the same even though when someone is in the middle of turmoil, this is hard for them to believe.

'Think' is a reminder to think before we speak. A preacher once said: 'Your tongue is in a wet place, and it can slip easily'.

Author Harriett Jackson Brown Jr said: 'Swallowing angry words before you say them is better than having to eat them afterwards.'[15] Thinking before I spoke and managing my anger was something I had to learn to do, and it changed my life for the better.

# CHAPTER TWENTY
## Tentacles of Addiction

Addiction in myriad forms is seeping insidiously into many people's lives, from the young to the old.

Cocaine Anonymous is a relatively new 12-step recovery group. Groups like these are growing like mushrooms all over Ireland such is the demand for them. So, what does that tell us about the cocaine crisis on our doorstep? Drugs are available in every village and through the letterbox by post of any home from the Internet.

Cannabis is regarded as a harmless drug, but unfortunately, it can cause psychosis, memory loss, concentration issues and impaired judgement, etc.

Gambling is taking lives all over the country through suicide. People who had everything to live for but end up as gambling addicts feel as though they have no way out of the silent hell that these people find themselves living in. Unfortunately, gambling addiction is set to continue with easy access to it on the Internet through the use of smartphones, and it is encouraged via the huge amount of advertising these companies can afford to do, including on TV. It is made to look like a lot of fun, which will appeal to younger audiences, too. Payday loans and free access to credit cards, etc., also make it more accessible. The gambling companies do not care about you or I or your family members. They only care about hooking you into their world with free bets, etc., because they know that once an addict starts gambling, they cannot stop.

Bookies are often the best buildings in the town, and they are in every town in Ireland. They are equipped with everything you may need to gamble all day without having to leave the premises.

Recovering from this type of addiction takes a great deal of self-discipline as, like alcohol, it is everywhere. A Gamblers Anonymous member said of gambling: 'It's only a problem when money can't fix it.'

Alcohol is sold in every nook and corner of the country because shop owners believe that if they do not sell alcohol, they may not draw in as many customers. If someone can't get out of their house to buy alcohol, they can phone their local delivery service, taxi or takeaway and get it delivered to their door with no regulations in place or no accountability for any adverse effects of this supply of alcohol to people who may already be drunk. I have witnessed alcohol being bought with a loaf of bread or maybe instead of a loaf of bread. It is so sad to watch young children with their parents at the supermarket when the adults are filling the shopping trolly with their stock of alcohol for the week. These parents are normalising a mood-altering chemical by combining it with weekly shopping. Alcohol affects every organ in the body. I smile when I hear young children taking their pledge for their confirmation at church to stay off alcohol until they are 18 and off drugs for life because alcohol is a drug. In the medical field, chemical dependency includes alcohol, which is often described as a gateway drug.

Many young people are caught up in the cycle of addiction in which sexual assaults and rape are commonplace for both men and women. The shame of this keeps them in active addiction to try and numb the trauma. Many people in addiction have experienced traumas in their lives and believe that if these events had not happened to them, they would not suffer from an addiction. I believe these are two separate issues as not everybody who has experienced traumatic events in their lives turns to drink or drugs. Only people with an addiction do so, and not everybody with addiction has had a traumatic experience in their life. Unfortunately, until addicts are clean and sober, they are not able to deal with their traumas.

If an addict does not reach out for recovery and commit themselves to it, the effects of addiction pass from one generation to the next. The same goes for the family members. In some cases, an alcoholic may stop drinking but not participate in recovery programmes, which means they will struggle to have contentment in their sobriety and often replace the alcohol, etc., with work or other activities. They could easily be triggered or tempted to return to drinking. It is possible for one person in recovery to help stop the cycle of addiction in their family, whether it is the addict or a family member. Some people who are reared with alcoholism make the grim resolution not to drink because of what they suffered during their childhood and the fear that if they took a drink, they might not be able to stop. They go through life congratulating themselves that they do not drink, but their behaviour may be every bit as destructive as an active drinker, if not sometimes worse. This is called 'the dry drunk syndrome'. Unless a person consumes alcohol and is able to stop, they do not know whether they would be likely to have a drinking problem or not.

Women cannot process or absorb alcohol as well as men. When women drink alcohol, they are more likely than men to have health problems such as cancer or liver damage. They are also more likely to experience family troubles, such as violence, as well as legal troubles, such as having their children placed in protective care. Women who have a history of breast cancer in their family should not drink alcohol as even small amounts can pose a risk of triggering breast cancer. Women who are planning to have a baby should not drink alcohol. When women drink alcohol during pregnancy, their children can suffer from lifelong problems such as foetal alcohol spectrum disorder and foetal alcohol syndrome. It is recommended that women and men should not drink more than 14 units of alcohol per week on a regular basis, which is about one-and-a-half bottles of wine and about six pints of beer.

# CHAPTER TWENTY-ONE
## Stop to Take Care of Yourself

Self-care is essential for you and your family members. If you don't look after yourself, you will not be able to look after anybody else. As demonstrated on an aircraft, you need to place the oxygen mask on yourself before helping others. Self-care and active addiction are total opposites. Not getting enough sleep, skipping meals, taking days off work due to worry, not attending to important matters, not going to the doctor or dentist when needed and not making time for relaxation, etc., can be all too familiar.

HALT is an acronym displayed in the recovery room. It is a reminder to stop and check in on how you are feeling. HALT: Am I hungry, angry or anxious, lonely or tired? If I am feeling any one of these, I must tend to that need. It's a bit like driving a car with a flat tyre or maybe two or three flat tyres and expecting it to function normally. I recognise in myself that when I am feeling tired, that's when the 'stinking thinking' and resentful thoughts come into my head. Now that I know this, I accept that it's the tiredness that is at work and let go of the negative thoughts.

Robin Norwood, author of *'Women Who Love Too Much'* [16], said that as a therapist, she would not make appointments with the family members of addicts if they were not willing to go to their own recovery meetings because they would not recover without them. I agree with her. Family members need these meetings, too, especially if their loved one is not yet in recovery. It is often the non-addict in the home that can do the most damage to their children. Many people are suffering needlessly because they are not willing to look at themselves. They can also be a misery to be around, like I was, and be avoided by others. I would much rather be included than avoided. Seeking support and accepting it is an act of self-care.

# CHAPTER TWENTY-TWO
## Right Time

When I was checking my emails, I saw a job advertised for a full-time addiction therapist in a private addiction clinic outside Ardee, Co. Louth. I had been invited to the opening of the clinic a couple of years earlier but had not been able to take time off work to attend. The funding for the Time Out Programme was coming to an end and I was keeping my eye out for some work to replace this. I sent the clinic my CV and an application form. I was offered an interview, and I accepted it out of curiosity to see what the place was like. When I found the clinic after getting lost a few times, I met the manager, and I hit it off with her straight away. It felt like I was talking to an old friend. The manager asked a member of staff to show me around Smarmore Castle. I liked the feel of the place and felt welcomed by the people I met.

I called in to visit my uncle on my way home. He was surprised to hear that I was even considering going to Ardee to work since part of my reason for selling the cottage was to be nearer to my workplace in Enniskillen. I had only moved there recently and had no internet connection. The manager of the clinic had told me that I would have to attend an online interview with the CEO sometime in the near future. When I got my internet set up, I tried to arrange the online call with the CEO, but when a time suited the CEO, it didn't suit me and vice versa. As a result, the interview never took place and so I carried on with my work in Co. Fermanagh.

At the end of March, while I was at work, an employee of Castle Craig private clinic in Scotland phoned me to ask me to check my emails as there was a job offer in the inbox. The post was based at another of the European group's rehabilitation clinics: Smarmore

Castle Drug and Alcohol Rehab in Ardee. Since the house that I moved to required work to revamp, having a secure monthly income seemed attractive while I could simultaneously gain the experience of working in a clinic that gave people a medically managed detox before their counselling began.

I took the job and once again found myself staying away from my home during the week, returning on a Friday evening. I'd leave again on Sunday evening and attend a recovery meeting on my way back to Ardee. It was because of this commitment that I was able to earn enough to get all the major things done to my house. My plan was to stay in that job for two years, but all the work in the house cost more than I expected, so I stayed for three years instead. I got promoted to a specialist therapist to work with the family of the person in rehab, but sadly, due to Covid 19, we never got it off the ground. I loved my work in Smarmore Castle, and I met a lot of lovely people there from all over Ireland, the UK and Europe.

The coronavirus pandemic changed everything suddenly. Job security was shaky. The health and well-being of our clients were under threat with the need for the 'Twelve Steps'[1] of recovery programme meetings increasing, but for the first time in history, there were no face-to-face meetings. We had to use online meeting rooms. We will never take things for granted after this pandemic.

I spent the summer of 2020 working from home due to being in one of the high-risk categories. I had decided to hand in my notice at the end of August, and despite the pandemic, I carried on with my decision. Work was still being carried out at my house, so I was busy with that, too. Sadly, my manager and good friend Mary Curtis passed away two days later after battling an illness.

# CHAPTER TWENTY-THREE
## One Day at a Time

It was my dream to move back to Fermanagh to set up my private practice at home, sharing with others who are in addiction and recovery the tools I used to help and heal myself. I feel privileged to be able to do the work I do and, through it, to meet so many wonderful people on their journey to a better life. A life that we all deserve. Online meeting rooms became the way people connected during lockdown and are now a part of everyday life that have enabled me to help people in many places.

I enjoy every minute of a much slower pace of life in Fermanagh. I love my home and being able to live and work in it. My life journey has led me here. A life filled with love, loss, lessons, changes, challenges, hope, determination, perseverance, independence and hard work. Now, I am able to use all of the experiences and knowledge that have shaped me to help other people. Looking back, what seemed like one setback after another was really one gift after another, enriching me to benefit others. My higher power had been guiding me all along into this beautiful destiny I could never have imagined as that 10-year-old girl playing in the wee room upstairs in my family home in Monaghan. I may not have ventured too far physically, living now in the neighbouring county to my first home, but emotionally I have travelled far beyond the bounds of known and chartered territory.

Addiction can creep up on anyone, but everyone dealing with addiction has just as much willpower inside as I do. I am an ordinary person, but I found something extraordinary inside myself. This ability to find something extraordinary lies in everyone. It's a strength that can be found deep within each and every one of us to create change, to transform a life from the depths of despair to one of joy.

I once felt lost and broken, but I fixed myself. Anything that becomes broken can be fixed, whether that be a mind or a heart. It takes self-love, self-care and determination to heal yourself and a belief that you are worth the effort. You have just as much right and opportunity to lead a fulfilling life as I do. Your life is as precious as everyone else's and is a gift. Maybe you just haven't finished unwrapping that gift yet to find the wonders waiting within.

You have the strength inside you to rise like a phoenix from the ashes of addiction and codependency into new heights of freedom and happiness. Find it within you. Many years of overcoming obstacles enabled me to forge a new landscape for myself with a brighter horizon.

Like me, you can become the architect of a better future, one step at a time, one day at a time.

# References

1.  Al-Anon Family Groups (1996) *Al-Anon's Twelve Steps.* Virginia: Al-Anon Family Group Headquarters, Inc.

2.  UK Rehab: https://www.uk-rehab.com/addiction/how-addiction-affects-others/

3.  Al-Anon Family Groups (2004) *Blueprint for Progress – Al Anon's Fourth Step Inventory.* Virginia: Al-Anon Family Group Headquarters, Inc.

4.  Brown, B. (2010) *The Gifts of Imperfection.* Minnestota: Hazelden.

5.  Brown, B.: https://brenebrown.com/videos/ted-talk-listening-to-shame/

6.  Brown, B. (2021) *Atlas of the Heart: Mapping Meaningful Connection and the Language of Human Experience.* Manhattan: Random House.

7.  Real, T. (1998) *I Don't Want to Talk about it: Overcoming the Secret Legacy of Male Depression.* New Jersey: Prentice Hall & IBD.

8.  Winter, C. (2023) *The Twelve Roles In A Dysfunctional Family Explained.* A Conscious Rethink: https://www.aconsciousrethink.com/19489/dysfunctional-family-roles

9.  Beattie, M. (2023) *Codependent No More: How to Stop Controlling Others and Start Caring for Yourself.* London: Bluebird.

10. Alinsky, Saul D. (2010) *Rules for Radicals: A Pragmatic Primer for Realistic Radicals.* London: Vintage, p.21.

11. Byrne, R. (1994) *The Secret.* New York: Simon & Schuster.

12. Hay, Louise L. (1984) *You Can Heal Your Life.* California: Hay House.

13. Lutzer, Erwin W. (1997) *Putting Your Past Behind You: Finding Hope for Life's Deepest Hurts.* Chicago: Moody Publishers.

14. Al-Anon Family Groups (1968) *One Day at a Time in Al-Anon.* Virginia: Al-Anon Family Group Headquarters, Inc.

15. Jackson Brown, Jr, H. (2007) *The Complete Life's Little Instruction Book: 1,560 Suggestions, Observations, and Reminders on How to Live a Happy and Rewarding Life.* Tennessee: Thomas Nelson.

16. Norwood, R. (2004) *Women Who Love Too Much.* Warwickshire: *Arrow*.

# Recommended Reading

Adams, M., Ph.D. (2017) *Silently Seduced, Revised & Updated: When Parents Make Their Children Partners, 2nd revised edition.* Florida: Health Communications Inc.

Al-Anon Family Groups (2015) *Courage to Change - One Day at a Time in Al Anon II.* Virginia: Al-Anon Family Group Headquarters, Inc.

Al-Anon Family Groups (2020) *Hope for Today.* Virginia: Al-Anon Family Group Headquarters, Inc.

Beattie, M. (1990) *The Language of Letting Go: Daily Meditations on Codependency: Daily Meditations for Codependents (Hazelden Meditation Series).* Minnesota: Hazelden FIRM.

Brown, B. (2017), *Braving the Wilderness: The Quest for True Belonging and the Courage to Stand Alone.* London: Vermilion.

Brown, B. (2018) *Dare to Lead: Brave Work. Tough Conversations. Whole Hearts.* New York: Random House.

Brown, B. (2007) *I Thought It Was Just Me (but it isn't): Making the Journey from "What Will People Think?" to "I Am Enough".* New York: Penguin.

Brown, B. (2015) *Rising Strong.* London: Vermilion.

Cameron, J. (2020) *The Artist's Way: A Course in Discovering and Recovering Your Creative Self.* London: Profile Books.

Norwood, R. (2015), *Daily Meditations for Women Who Love Too Much.* Warwickshire: Arrow.

Norwood, R. (2015) *Letters from Women Who Love Too Much.* Warwickshire: Arrow.

O'Connor, R. (2021) *When It Is Darkest: Why People Die by Suicide and What We Can Do to Prevent It*. London: Vermilion.

Ruiz, D. M. (2018) *The Four Agreements: A Practical Guide to Personal Freedom (A Toltec Wisdom Book)*. California: Amber-Allen Publishing, Incorporated.

Todd, B. P. and Sara S. (2018) *Drop the Rock: Removing Character Defects - Steps Six and Seven*. Minnesota: Hazelden Trade.

Tolle, E. (2009) *A New Earth - Create A Better Life*. London: Penguin.

Winfrey, O. (2017) *The Wisdom of Sundays: Life-Changing Insights from Super Soul Conversations*. New York: Flatiron Books.

www.ingramcontent.com/pod-product-compliance
Lightning Source LLC
Chambersburg PA
CBHW071537120626
46550CB00006B/2487